Autumn Grasses

Autumn Grasses

poems

MARGARET GIBSON

)|(LOUISIANA STATE UNIVERSITY PRESS   BATON ROUGE   2003

Cloth
12 11 10 09 08 07 06 05 04 03
5 4 3 2 1
Paper
12 11 10 09 08 07 06 05 04 03
5 4 3 2 1

Designer: Barbara Neely Bourgoyne
Typeface: Arcana Manuscript (display); Adobe Minion (text)
Printer and binder: Thomson-Shore, Inc.

LIBRARY OF CONGRESS CATALOGING-IN-PUBLICATION DATA:
Gibson, Margaret.
Autumn grasses : poems / Margaret Gibson.
    p. cm.
ISBN 0-8071-2858-9 (alk. paper) — ISBN 0-8071-2859-7 (pbk. : alk. paper)
I. Title.
PS3557.I1916 A96 2003
811'.54—dc21
                                    2002151094

The author gratefully acknowledges the editors of the following publications, in which the poems listed first appeared, sometimes in slightly different form: *Artful Dodge:* "Equinox," "Naming It," "Wild Duck"; *Common Review:* "The Giant Snowball"; *Connecticut Review:* "Girl with Violin," "Mt. Fuji on the Lid of the Writing Box," "Summer Birds and Flowers (II)," "Woman at Her Writing Table"; *Georgia Review:* "The Bobcat"; *Hollins Critic:* "Boy Juggling"; *Iowa Review:* "Bamboo Yards at Kyōbashi," "Noh Robe"; *Iron Horse Literary Review:* "Flock of Cranes," "Kinryuzan Temple at Asakusa," "Poppies," "Summer Garden"; *Margie:* "From the Brothel Window Darkening Fields at Sunset"; *Prairie Schooner:* "A Chinese Beauty Considers the Peony," "Woman Resting on a Bundle of Kindling"; *River Oak Review:* "Coming and Going," "Round and Round the Entry Screen"; *Shenandoah:* "Autumn Grasses," "Autumn Ivy," "Korin's Bridge"; *Southern Humanities Review:* "Marriage Bed (I)," "Marriage Bed (III)"; *Southern Review:* "Evening Mist," "The Great Wave at Kanagawa," "The Hag Ibaragi," "Sweetfish in a Spring Current," "Toko's Cat"; *Square One:* "Poem Beginning with an Image of Fireflies"; *Tampa Review:* "Gift," "Marriage Bed (II)," "Scene from the *Tales of Ise.*"

The author is also grateful to the editors of the following electronic magazines and magazine Web sites, which posted the following poems: *Blackbird:* "Birds and Flowers (I)," "Drifting Boat," "Fox Fire at the Changing Tree," "Next Morning Letter"; *Tricycle:* "Beginner's Mind," "Bellflowers for the Tokonoma," "The Gathering at the Orchid Pavilion," "Japanese White-Eyes," "Summer," "The Temptation of Prince Siddhartha," "Today Also," "The Zen Master Seiōgyū."

This book is for my grandchildren
Henry Van Kirk McKain and
Lucy Jane Hill McKain

From wonder to wonder
Existence opens . . .

A storm wind blows
Out from among the grasses
A full moon grows

Contents

Autumn Grasses

AUTUMN GRASSES

In fields of bush clover and hay-scent grass
the autumn moon takes refuge
The cricket's song is gold

Zeshin's loneliness taught him this

Who is coming?
What will come to pass, and pass?

Neither bruise nor sweetness nor cool air
not-knowing
knows the way

And the moon?
Who among us does not wander, and flare
and bow to the ground?

Who does not savor, and stand open
if only in secret

taking heart in the ripening of the moon?

(Shibata Zeshin, Autumn Grasses, *two-panel screen)*

NOH ROBE

Slip it on, and learn

how the mind fabricates
itself in leafy
bamboo and young pine

how a woman

for her lover unpins
a silken tent
her night-black hair

Slip it on, and follow

the one thread of her many lives
dwelling no-where—
with no prayer to lift into the night

yes, borne along

through the worn-down
mountains,
into the depths of the human heart

Wearing only

the rain song silence in the pines
along the river
Wearing only the verdant

brocade of bamboo

(Karaori, Edo period)

TOKO'S CAT

Behind the screen
the brush-tip of the cat's supple tail

softly flicks

In one skillful stroke
the iris of each jade green eye

narrows to a slit

Such concentration
the spider is the only jewel in the lotus

And the cat, a tensile readiness to pounce

attuned to the least
decibel of silence that might be sounded

as the spider glides across emptiness

Who is Toko? Only a still mind can
relish as precisely

Thus the whiskers, thus the claws

Thus the sprigs on the silken scarf
knotted casually

about the neck of this pampered cat—

in whose heart Toko has recognized
a tiger's

gravity and grace

(*Toko,* Cat and Spider, *album leaf*)

SWEETFISH IN A SPRING CURRENT

Slipping completely through

No effort in the way
they breast the swifts and ravels

On the mountain azaleas
beads of clear water

In the distance, a hum of bees

Affixed to the rock-face
that borders the brook

are blue abrasions of lichen

They neither thaw nor float
They thrive in the shadows

Blossoms beyond naming

they are like sorrows
that slip into the heart

without hurry, impervious

(*Maruyama Ōkyo,* Sweetfish in a
Spring Current, *hanging scroll*)

WOMAN AT HER WRITING TABLE

She is the pause
before

the word

the harbor
before

wind—

a bare limb
polished

by the rigor of rain

In early spring
an ache—

then the tremor of a lithe

green leaf
shaped as a fan is

Ginkgo

She dips her brush
in ink

and roots the word

in the melting
snow

(*Komai Genki,* Chinese Beauty, *hanging scroll*)

THE GATHERING AT THE ORCHID PAVILION

Beneath a single moon

the trees fill their branches
brush-tip green

A fresh branch of lightning
whitens the orchard

The roof of the pavilion is a mist
blue as the far mountain

Mist also
the borders of the poets' sleeves

They are gathered to greet
the spring wind

that shadows
the empty scroll before them

with flowers in the sky

The ox-bow bend in the river is blue
the cloth on the table red

The bird of the other world is singing

They are old, yes. They will die—
but why sit in the ashes

and wail
and bang the empty iron pot?

A musky scent of woodsearth
and orchids

flares the nostrils

(Ike Taiga, The Gathering at the Orchid Pavilion, *six-panel screen)*

    for Kuge

BEGINNER'S MIND

Roshi has opened the absolute eye
a kind of spotting scope

to study the grackles at his April feeder

To the casual observer
the grackle is raucous, clumsy

The sort you can count on to spill seed

its cry a wheezy *ka-shee* or *zweesh*
toneless, testy

as it sets the bird feeder rocking
like a morbid drunkard

gwalfing the swill down fast

gwalfing and swiveling
the neck sideways and backward

on guard for the Cooper's

that all winter's been swooping down on
smaller birds at the feeder

Roshi remembers

a mound of scattered black feathers
on snow. But now

the sun shimmers free of the clouds

and the shroud of the grackle glows
purple, a twilight plum

deepening to a shade of satin, black

spangled with citrines and peridots
A night sky

receding into the pupil of the Buddha's eyeball

Roshi bows. He has seen the Buddha
And he keeps on seeing Buddha

as the sun dulls

into cloud smear, a spit of rain
Old ink and rust now the grackle's shroud

Roshi bows—this bird *also* Buddha!

JAPANESE WHITE-EYES

On a bend of bamboo
three birds one body

One bows to the earth
one to wind

One carries the moon
a dewdrop

white in its eye

(Kitagawa Utamaro, Japanese White-Eyes,
colored wood-block print, from Momo-chidori*)*

BOY JUGGLING

He is poised
in open
space

a balanced stance
attuned
to any tremor

His upturned hands
are the wings
of delicate seedlings

nearly released

But the pull of the earth
we feel it
in his feet

Slow now, steady
he flings into orbit
red spirals

snail shells or fiddle heads
snapped from their stalks
Nothing to cling to

nowhere to root

And they shimmer
in the clean
rinsed air

To toss and breathe
to concentrate
suspend and move

all at once—
this is his special
failing

He cannot halt the spheres

nor turn to see
just there, behind him
in the still water

the narrow flute
of the wren's
tail, its tilt

Nor the branch
that ravels
and unravels

in the sky of the puddle

Nor heed
the invisible source
that bids the bird rest

*(attributed to Katsushika Hokusai, from
an album of ninety-seven sketches)*

THE ZEN MASTER SEIŌGYŪ

At first glance
one smiles, or has to laugh—

he's riding *backwards* on an ox
this old monk

of the Northern Song

The ox is robust and mild
well-muscled

And the monk?

He has tethered to one horn of the ox
a branch of flowering peony

From the pucker of his cheek
we surmise that he is also smiling

Who knows the way?

Travel the slope of his shoulders
the calm curve of his back

The road, however dark or long
is brushed by

the springtime shadow of petals

(Kano Naizen, The Zen Master Seiōgyū,
one of a pair of hanging scrolls)

     for Lysbet

FROST IN MAY

What might have been
silken

scarves of green
light

wind has
littered to the ground

Dry scrolls
black

as fox scat
Husks

in the morgue
of spring

the tanager
returns to

Red body
black wings

BAIKA

When Baika meets Roshi in the rutted dirt road
at Shinagawa

how does she show her true face

the one before she rouged her mouth
that plum pip

or penciled the wings of a gull on her forehead?

On the painted fan she holds open before
her white throat

there is no wind in the tiny portrait
of waterfront and harbor

How empty is her boat? you ask. How long has she
sheltered in the silky "bay of sleeves"?

She takes on passengers—that is her calling

however boundless the sky
however single the moonlit hand Roshi

holds out to her. He bows, she smiles—
she has prepared for this meeting

removing from her sleeve

a small box, trussed and gilded with ribbon
She offers it

to that single hand, which holds the power

of rain and wind in the blossoming
plum trees

Inside the box he finds a dried crescent

knotty and black, flecked with
the blue of the Buddha's eyeball

It is *plum blossom in snow, just one branch*
It is also just what it is

a dried dog turd

Roshi howls, he barks, he bows nine times
then snaps his sleeves

striding off under the boundless, empty spring sky

(Kitagawa Utamaro, Courtesan Holding a Fan, *wood-block print,
from the series "Beauties of the Southern Provinces")*

KORIN'S BRIDGE

Blue iris against a sky icon gold—
and the bridge to summer's silken temple

is sturdy
Plain planks one might actually walk on

Who does not
wish the body to be like this?

A durable plenitude. Well-traveled
(Bring your face closer)

(Breathe slowly against my skin)
And fragrant

(Ogata Korin, Irises by an Eight-Planked Bridge,
one of a pair of six-panel screens)

MARRIAGE BED (I)

As much sea as sky
the kimono spread on our bed

And I am, beloved

the persimmon moon
above you

hovering, ripe

Your rising from the dark sea
pleases me

the tail of the lobster tilted back

taut against your body
stiff with longing

Both of us held in the sound

of the sea's
constant breath, the sea as deep

as any reverie of what it's like

to swell, to sink
to ripen into the other, to meet

(Coverlet, Meiji period)

A CHINESE BEAUTY CONSIDERS
THE PEONY

If silence is a wall
the peony
is a doorway in that wall

I have given up the struggle to explain

Nourished by loss
whose nature
is to inhabit abundance

all night I turn my face
to that hard pillow
the moon

I open my legs to the dark

By day the sun unfolds
petal by petal
white-hot

The peony
yields
to the scent inside it

The peony does not
justify
or doubt itself

Whatever is bountiful

whatever is real
arises
in the center of such blooming

(*Komai Genki*, Chinese Beauty, *hanging scroll*)

SUMMER GARDEN

Now what is clamorous
quiets

What has been delayed
is granted

A fullness as compliant
as the glass bowl of water

with the light shining through

Three pink and white carp
suspended there

plump and tumescent
their gauzy fins barely flickering

like petals on a bloom only
just come open

An after-pulse, as after
the heat of love

The water is still, also the air
with its rambling plush

of roses and *passiflora*
heavily nodding above the bowl

As if a mirrory
spell were on the mind

letting what enters
enter, and double

then nod into lavish scent

(*Sō Shizan,* Summer Garden, *hanging scroll*)

POPPIES

Before the scroll
of poppies
in full midsummer flourish

you will perhaps think it strange

that I do not take refuge
in their profuse
ruddy festival

You ask if I can forgive, I can

Look how the artist has so
cleverly rendered
each early slim bud

A grievance, compact and potent

A green snake's head
pendant
on a crook of green stem

Split at midseam each one
will open, lifting
a scarlet

somersault of ruffled skirts

We cannot rouse from silence
the center
of the flower dark with seed

You ask if I am grateful, I do not know

After the white flash, left
to live as we could on the torn
earth, in the city rubble . . .

How could we have known

our children's small bodies
would bloody
with blossoms

rising heavily to the surface

nodding, as if called from the dark
Little bonfires
Dragon's tongues

Poppies

(Kitagawa Sōsetsu, Poppies, *hanging scroll)*

NEXT MORNING LETTER

Savoring each summer moment
lush and brief
I close my eyes to see

your white robe, falling open

as you call for your scroll
and ink stone, a brush
As your brush passes over the paper

my body shivers

How closely now you watch
at the open lattice
as your servant hurries away

the next morning letter

tethered to
a spray of clematis
whose blossoms will not open

until they reach me

In the wash basin
your face is
the bridge that spans

the floating world of dreams

Now you are yawning
Now you are reciting sutras
bowing to the wind

When the letter arrives

all the leaves of the maple
outside my window
are stirred

I read your words

just once, then once again
bringing my fingers
to my lips—my hair

tucked back behind one ear

On the dawn's trellis
the scent of clematis
Now smell your fingers
The petals of my body
gather in your empty arms

How shall I respond?
The cry of the stag
is so loud

the echo answers

from the empty mountains
as if it were a doe
I tell you only what you know

Clematis—the scent
of your teaching surrounds me
My empty arms fill
Come night, the fragrant petals
fall in a heap at my feet

(Kaigetsudō Doshin, Beauty Writing
a Letter, *hanging scroll)*

SUMMER

Blue morning glories
spilling on a golden ground
They say what I think

(Suzuki Kiitsu, Morning Glories,
one of a pair of six-panel screens)

SUMMER BIRDS AND FLOWERS (I)

Unrolling
the coiled scroll

enacts the momentary

sweeping down the midday sky
of small birds

on a draft from the distant
blue ravines

and mountain ridges

into the windy clearing
of summer's

middle distance, so luminous
and near

it's easy to ignore

given the distraction
of hollyhocks

and the stalks of amber iris
that steeply

lean into the emptiness

that borders
the tended garden path

Any fear of what imperils
and impends

is thereby tempered—

the tidal and jagged line
of the far mountains

merely an artful
mapping of the birds'

arc of flight

And such a glimmer of gaiety
as they dip and swoop

with unguarded ease
into the inseparable

immensity

my heart stops now
as I think of it

(Shikibu Terutada, Summer Birds and Flowers,
one of a pair of hanging scrolls)

SUMMER BIRDS AND FLOWERS (II)

I don't know just why
but mountains rest on the bend
of a grass blade, blue
A bird in a narrow mask
scalds the air with its scolding

I take refuge in
second-bloom roses, asters
tiny volcanoes
of sun in their ripe centers
It's nearly over, summer

A scroll on a wall
is an open window—one
simply looks and looks
Who dies? Who dies? Who suffers?
Who's born in this absolute

stillness? *No one's home*
But now the tempter steals in
I don't know just why
Perhaps it's always here
softly scolding, the old wish

to be good, be good
Just this spring, drunk with its scent
spellbound by the need
to be more near, I opened
the windows out, transparent

I would drink it in
all day, the heart of the world
And at dusk walked out
to find below the blunt glass
a bird, its eye white as milk

(Shikibu Terutada, Summer Birds and Flowers,
one of a pair of hanging scrolls)

THE BOBCAT

If a sandstorm can crouch
If each muscle

lynx-like, alert

can be an eye, and the eye
leap through

daylight to where light *is*

and at that speed—
If knowing

the *look* of silence

impeccable, unpracticed
is a carnal

pour up the hill and over

the lawn, emptying itself
into leaf-scent

and a slip of light

more rapidly than syllables
can link themselves

into speech—

then there was a *bobcat*
on the terrace

yes, a bobcat

bounding over the formal
garden we planted

with bushes called
blue mist

and with roses bred by an Englishman

who could anchor elusive
fragrance to wild stock and root it

But why should you believe me?

I scoffed at the hanging scroll
that showed

a civet cat, imperious

beneath a willow
and well-groomed camellias

Come here—

even now the stones beneath
my bare feet

retain vestiges

of a soft morning turned
suddenly trenchant

boreal, with a shearlike edge

POEM BEGINNING WITH
AN IMAGE OF FIREFLIES

All night, watching
those aerial embers
wink off and on

beneath the stars
in the meadowy
clearing around the pond

I try to scatter
the sparks
of my desire, every taste

each touch and trace
even the faintest fragrance
of my wanting you

But who would chasten
the fires of desire
must swim, come morning

in a weedy pond, as I do now
having left behind
my rings, my clothes

the house just now waking
in the welter of bird cry
Must turn aside from

the weeping beech
lichen gray in the mist
Must ignore the sun

burning off the mist
that conceals
the one bright pearl I'm after

Must forget *I'm* and *after*
pearl and *goal*
And go where light is

Around me like silk, like silt
the pond opens and closes
and I swim in circles

my fingertips brushing
frogbit, bottom sedge
and waterweed

Breath by breath I take on
the life of the old
muddy bass who outwits

all the sharp hooks
that have dangled before it
even the tiniest of enticements

And yes, smiling at this fine
conceit, taking refuge
as it fades into water and ripple

into the bubbles of my breath
Until, exhausted, I flip over
on my back, floating now

into a scented commonwealth
of pond lilies—astonished
to see high overhead

a pond of sky, invisible fathoms
measureless air
that only seems to be rimmed

by the billowy crowns
of the oaks
that edge the clearing

Whatever once I wanted
whatever once I was
is now just

this unguarded light, without
beginning or end
As it floats

in me, I float in it
so empty, nacreous, and bright
I cannot tell in which

pond above or pond below
not one, not two
there are floating now

tip-to-tip attached
two green dragonflies
taking their full ease

GIRL WITH VIOLIN

Barely visible
like Lady Ukifune
who lived on moonlight
and mist, as *heart dwindlingly*
I have hidden from the Source

Or like the young girl
brought to the Court uncultured
I've withdrawn behind
the kicho, just a fragrant
shadow, living book to book

Is it better now
(you ask) in my schoolgirl cloak
with a schoolgirl bow
in my hair, serenading
the crescent moon as it dims?

Don't think I practice
dutiful music, lost in
measures not my own
What would echo accomplish?
Oh, I am a crazy girl!

Hear the violin
as it lengthens my true voice
and the dragon girl
wells in my heart, her wisdom
sharp-rooted, radiant, free

(Kaburagi Kiyokata, Morning Dew, *frontispiece illustration for a work of romantic fiction, 1903)*

MARRIAGE BED (II)

You want me to tell you the truth?

There's a bed
spacious enough for a host of lovers

and you lie in it

only mildly aware of your hunger
and thirst

You want his arms around you?

I tell you
he's under your skin already

he's the taste in your mouth

And the soft breath in your ear?
You've mistaken it

for death's cool syllables

They are the words you never
learned to unsay

in the intimate transfer of breath

tongue to tongue
You are old now, you are old

And still it's not too late!

Lo, I am with you always
is not enough

unless you can see within

from the crown of the bloom
to the muck it roots in

See intimately, directly

and your whole body
pulses into sunrise, as gold

as the storehouse of pollen

in the lily that opens
as morning spreads wide

Heavy with perfume, wet with dew

(Coverlet, Meiji period)

TAGASODE (WHOSE SLEEVES?)

A smell of steam
the scent of flowering trees

If the kimonos could only
whisper

what they have learned
to savor

The friction of silk
on skin, the fragrances

(Six-panel screen, Edo period)

KIMONO WITH CRICKET CAGES IN MOONLIGHT

Wearing this, I know
how Izumi Shikibu
(to meet her lover)
hid behind the sudare
Windowpanes of soft white silk

Her sleeves wet with tears
her skin a sort of twilight
The soul hides itself
working in the dark of day
or nights, when the moon is gauze

Her passion? Tactful
She lay on her lonely bed
too awake, blowing
words on the embers of stars
wondering, What *is* the heart?

Perhaps a wild swan
lifting beyond the mountains
to the sun? The Prince
comes to her, meticulous
in his shuttered palanquin

So much depends on
the color of silk, on scent
A tachibana
flower in May. In autumn
red, flying leaves. The crescent

moon slips like a comb
to the cold floor. And how shrill
the crickets! Even
with her hair unbound, her hands
pressed shrewdly against her ears

the cage of the heart
shimmers with their precise songs

(Kimono, Meiji period)

EVENING MIST

Far from the dust of the city
he has made his way, looking beyond

to where flowers are not, nor tinted leaves

And come to this solitary hut, this abode
of emptiness among the dunes

the light of autumn waning, quince and gold

Such a flimsy shelter—that is its beauty, composed
by binding the toppled grasses of the field

He sits with his back to the distant sea

melancholy, tired of living in the body
taking refuge

in the light all things fall into

He does not notice the slender doe
lift her head from grazing the field, her taut muscles

trembling, her neck

curved back toward the eager buck behind her
as he prepares to mount

Who can bear it, happiness . . . unhappiness?

Inside the hut, the kettle sings
like a cataract muffled by clouds, like a rainstorm

or a river that runs to the sea

and empties into it, vast and soundless
Even if he turned and gazed beyond the horizon

he couldn't see across to the opposite shore

Even if he could, he'll not easily forget her dark hair
languid along his thigh, nor his tongue

in the salt savor and chambered privacy of her flesh

its colors of ocher and old ivory made more
present by her absence here

Humbly the kettle sings, of tea green and frothy

In a moment he will bend low
and pass through the narrow door of the hut

as one enters the presence of grief or joy more fully

by attending to what is simple, ceremonial
The kettle is angular, the cup round

Light slants in from the west

On the tokonoma he has put a single reed
in a vase the color of mist

(Ishiyama Moroka, Eight Views of the Tale of Genji, *hand scroll)*

SCENE FROM *THE TALES OF ISE*

From the way he stands
one can tell

he is used to command, his judgments
swift, incisive

A warrior cries, *Hoo-awgh!*
as the blade slides in. Or, *Hawgh!*

And perhaps he *has* been too abrupt
this aristocrat

erect at the verge of the stubborn road
in his gorgeous silk trousers

and long-tailed jacket of intricate
cloth, cerulean and gold

He has a groom to tend his horse
His saddle is waxed and supple

But his beloved has said: *Don't come*

Unpracticed in the ways of the heart
his heart, for now

is heat and waste, mirage
and great distance

He doubts that he can attain it
a heart deep as sky, compliant

And so he has entrusted to desolation
all his longing

and to the pilgrim passing by
in his dusty sandals

his willingness to wait, obedient
to silence

Nor does he say, *Forgive me*

Already he has begun to climb
the steep road beyond

self-pity, beyond entreaty
with its sharp edge of contrivance, excuse

The heart of the pilgrim is empty
spacious

Light, before light
breaks open

I am not what you *think*
says the heart

(Tawaraya Sōtatsu, Scene from Ise Monogatari,
album leaf mounted as a hanging scroll)

BELLFLOWERS FOR THE TOKONOMA

Ripening with wind
now the kimono billows
and bows on the line
strung between the fragrant boughs
of the cryptomeria

Only the wind knows
how silk absorbs the rich tang
of tender cedar
Only the wind knows which bell
rings within the carpenter

who hews the cedar
and shaves it thin as parchment
As for me, only
wind leaves the heart unguarded
enough—each fitful shifting

each shudder of sun
spills into my upturned hands
My longing (you say)
is the scent that wells and wells
as one fills a basket with fruit

or a brush with inks
bruise black as these bellflowers
Note the delicate
stems as they float in the wind
that is faithfully yoking

flower and shadow
in the panel Korin made
So fierce and kind was
his suffering, it summoned
from his aching heart

the taste of the wind
as it blooms over water
The heat of the sun

as it rises *inside* wood
Inside the fragrant body

(Ogata Korin, Chinese Bellflowers,
one of a pair of hanging panels)

TODAY ALSO

The empty mirror
you left on the windowsill
brings the sky inside

MIMIZUKU

This owl
has heard it all before

Enough amorous cooing!

Fluff the feathers, preen?
Why bother hooing

Watch its gold eyes
(urbanely)

blink

(Kitagawa Utamaro, Scops Owl,
colored wood-block print, from
Momo-chidori*)*

YAMAUBA TO KINTOKI

It's true
I am wanton

Why then
do you pout

the prodigious
nose

of your Tengu
mask

at a phallic
tilt?

I have bared
one breast

You raise
one finger

Is it
our true nature

your mask
lays bare?

My wet
tongue

flicks
my lower lip

How can I help
but smile

covering my
mouth

with the back
of my hand

curling my
fingers

into an intimate
tunnel

Never mind your
gray hair

and attainments
Every man

is a lusty
nursling

every woman
a wet nurse

Come get

(*Kitagawa Utamaro*, Yamauba
with Kintoki in a Tengu Mask,
wood-block print)

THE HAG IBARAGI

The shadow she casts is a dragon's
Her breath hot piss through snow

Eyes: a civet cat's at night, molten amber

She hunts the bare ground of the heart
bitter hours in Old Japan

when the royal halls give audience

to the wind and hungry ghosts
crowd the bed

as if it were a banquet table

She gnaws equally on the hearts of
men and women, especially

young women at Court, the lovely

daughters of powerful Lords
Kohyoé or Ko Uma

Dignified flowers, who bind their
long black hair with white chords and saishi

Lady Saisho, Lady Koshosho, Lady Hyoé

their billowy silks tastefully accented
by sea waves and chrysanthemums

silver cranes and pines

Into their dreams, into the grape and
scarlet rags of dawn, Ibaragi flings

the bloodied stump of her raw red arm

Shameless, entirely shameless
face to face with men, she has wielded

the sword, she has taken their blows

Who knows the heart's rapture
knows also its merciless hunger

The heart, wrote Lady Murasaki Shikibu,
is *invisible, dreadful*

She must have noticed on the polished
palace floor the yellowed bone

that slid from Ibaragi's hair, white
as gristle, coarse as salt

Or felt the fish-scale rasp of Ibaragi's tongue
scorch her heart

Asleep beneath the face cloth, her head
at rest on her writing case of lacquered gold

she must have seen Ibaragi

hitch her bloody skirts and lick her parts
wagging her haunches

at the moon as it lingers

in the fields of silver dew, the same moon
the ladies gather to admire

resplendent in white behind the shielding misu

(Shibata Zeshin, The Hag Ibaragi, *from a pair
of two-panel screens)*

THE TAO OF LOVE

Wu-wei, wu-wei
the robin's song

weighs heavy on the heart
What to do, what to do . . .

Flowers fall
their full-blown petals

wet with dew

(Kitagawa Utamaro, Japanese Robin and
Chrysanthemums, *colored wood-block print,
from* Momo-chidori*)*

FOX WEDDING

Here is elegance
and gelded
pomp

Here also music
and incense
Banners

and the feckless calm
of compromise

But you can't fool a fox, no way

They see the shogun's
pantomime of power
his royal

bride's inaugural ennui

And they lift their fiery tails
They hoist them
high

Grizzled torches
that peel off
a comet-train of sparks

Shame on you! Shame!

Who cannot give yourselves
to an honest
rapture

to the ardent, chaste bright flame!

(Ukita Ikkei, Tale of a Strange Marriage,
hand scroll)

MARRIAGE BED (III)

Abandoned, yet
after all our promises

I still call you to my bed

I know we have no
future

That's the price we pay

for starving our delight
In the end

my troubled love

has turned to fear
and I lie

in the palm of its hand

just before it closes
into a fist

Remembering how once

just once, you peeled
a ripened quince

and offered it

crescent by crescent
even after

I'd turned away my head

(Coverlet, Meiji period)

FROM THE BROTHEL WINDOW
DARKENING FIELDS AT SUNSET

Hiroshige has given us sky
in bands of colored
light—at the height, cold indigo

then a broad sweep of blue
fading into the luminous
emptiness of white

And nearer the darkening fields

the brilliant glow and shed-blood
red of the sun
Across the evening fields

a line of pilgrims, revelers
returns from the shrine
where they prayed for prosperity

And why not?

Who doesn't want to be happy?
They have been
in the presence of the gods

They have bowed and chanted
and bowed—
now they can laugh and sing

and bow to the forces of pleasure

On the windowsill of the brothel
there's a bowl for washing
and a cloth left casually there

by one of the women, who has gazed
off into the blue
middle distance of the sky

narrowing her eyes

On the sill, near where she stood
a white cat
studies the fields below the window

and her ears twitch—perhaps
she hears the pilgrims
singing? From the inner room's

familiar, ragged cries

she has turned her back
Detached and
somehow wiser than her kind

in a few more lifetimes perhaps
the cat will be
Franz Kafka, no stranger

to suffering, moved to chide

or comfort himself thus:
You may hold yourself back
from the pain of the world—

you are free to do that
But perhaps
this holding back

is the one suffering

you might be able to avoid
For Hiroshige
the evening merely darkens

and comes down, its lush
crimson canceled by
the black lacquer of a boundless

box, whose lid falls silently shut

(Andō Hiroshige, Visitors to the Tori-no-Machi Festival,
from the series "One Hundred Famous Views of Edo")

BAMBOO YARDS AT KYŌBASHI

Along the great wooden bridge at Kyōbashi
the pilgrims straggle home

footsore, quiet now, and sleepy

The city's cache of bamboo
is sufficient, their prayers have been confident

The future is assured

They are alive
They are safe, even happy

The moon

rises without comment
over the steep ramparts and spires

of bundled bamboo

For the laborer below, moonlight
is only more light to work by

He poles his barge along the bright river

What he thinks, no one asks
What he thinks falls away as smoothly

as the runnel of river water

that slides down the pole he lifts
holds aloft for a moment

then sinks into the shining river

(Andō Hiroshige, Bamboo Yards at Kyōbashi, *wood-block
print, from the series "One Hundred Famous Views of Edo")*

THE TEMPTATION OF PRINCE SIDDHARTHA

Think you're alone?

Don't open your eyes, nor
close them

Be neither *for* nor *against*

Yes, there is smoke in the wind
and somewhere

a windrow of red maple leaves
is the lovers' only bed

But if there's the full moon behind you
if below, the earth

If you've already swallowed
the vast sea and sky

there's no room for the roaring torrent
of skulls

The brawny
blue demon, the warrior in red diapers

waving his sword—*whom can they kill?*

In the pool of clear water
before him

no image of the Illumined One
returns the gaze

(Temptation of Prince Siddhartha, *hand scroll, from an
illustrated version of* The Sutra of Cause and Effect)

THE GREAT WAVE AT KANAGAWA

Above you and your flimsy fishing boat

About to plummet
on your bald, uncovered head

the swelling heave, the sea, the tsunami

You will die, you know this

but it takes this wave

to make you bow your head
your heart, your whole life

And all for nothing

Nothing arrests the dark-held wave

Nothing quells Mt. Fuji's steadfast light

as it brightens the gunwale
and the dripping oars

The wave unrolls its readiness to kill you

No choice left

No safety, no rescue, no excuse

And no refuge but going into it
Entirely listening

to the sound of the wave on Mt. Fuji

Hearing in the marrow of your bones

waterlogged and heavy

only the sound of letting your breath out slow
as the steep wave snows down

In such extended motion

you dance and dissolve in the seethe

Much as flotsam rides the steep

cascade of foam and water
Melting into one cry

as the empty boats break up

and rush

over the edge of the boundless

*(Katsushika Hokusai, wood-block print, from
the series "Thirty-Six Views of Mt. Fuji")*

AUTUMN JOY

The deer stands perfectly still

The long black snake
is a motionless

swirl at the burrow hole
all the morning ready

The sky is blue
this hammock no other than Indra's

net, shining now
in the hum of bees that alights

on the sedum we call
autumn joy

One by one the leaves yellow
loosening their hold

on the mind still in love
with birth and death

You are no different from me
fuel in the bonfire

that reduces the gods of plenty
and poverty to ash

They are one and the same
god, after all

JAPANESE CHRYSANTHEMUMS

And what's more, the exquisite
moon-shaped fan

Hiroshige made
to fit his vision of chrysanthemums

in a mass of russet and gold
beneath the blue and white

checkered roof of the festive
market stall

is the same to me as, right now
the clouds

Immaculate rags
that polish the sky

Move the fan, or don't move it—
up the dirt path

comes a rare wind bearing
foolish Jittoku, sweeping

the path clear of wood chips and dust
Also Kanzan, with his madcap

songs and scrolls, his rags
and ratty ponytail

Both of them laughing at the moon
as it floats between

the heaving wings
of the geese flying south

(Andō Hiroshige, Japanese Chrysanthemums,
wood-block print)

EQUINOX

Overnight, rain
blackens the trunks of the maples

The hammock
is littered with gold leaves

I swim quickly through the pond's
cold black mirror

Beneath the lily pads
shadowy fish

are pulsing
their long, gauzy fins

MT. FUJI ON THE LID OF
THE WRITING BOX

The moon is full

Fresh snow
brightens the summit

Streaks of plum
still ripen the clouds

Their cries faintly white

wild geese
drift down to the pines

to the sandbars and the sea
ginkgo gold

I brush my fingers

lightly along the line
of hills

that swell and fall
in unison

swell and fall

The one body of the world
neither

magnified nor made
more small

by any word I say

*(Writing box, black lacquer with sprinkled gold
and mother-of-pearl inlay, nineteenth century)*

NAMING IT

A low sound. More clear when I do not
name it. *Dove*

the mind says anyway

Backlit, bright against a blue so clear
it resists greed altogether

the clouds are a cobbled path
into the sun's burning

the *stop-here* of the cedars
into ash and stars

There it is again. And again

Owls, I murmur—the way I say
stars, drawn more

to the black chasm between them

PRESQUE ISLE

Stone markers, ashes, the self—
I know we must consider these

But the lake is as mortal. And that is
why the earth seems to rest

in silent meditation, the leaves of the sun
blowing gold and claret and sherry

This white sand ridge, solid enough
to walk on, moving in truth like a cloud

If I could muster it, I'd be an unknowing
as winged, as seamless as these

flashes of scarlet intermittence you say are
woodpeckers, having constructed each one

from the hollow rattle of its call
and the pattern of black and white

and brilliant red that drills on the broken
baroque of these old oaks

Headstrong, momentary
they are what I cannot see for looking

But just look into those bald, black
imperturbable eyes—unblinking, passionless

There's the unknowable, *that's* what does
as it must, without thinking it, seeing everything

as it is, unlike nothing else, and God

AUTUMN IVY

Each leaf: a bright jewel, a hot coal

If orchards, they are ripe
If celebrations, brief

Two weathered ones are mottled
brown and green

They are broad wings gliding down
the hanging scroll

Hawks on a thermal

Soon we will sit by the window and watch
blue shadows

lengthen along the snowy fields

When he knew he was dying, he gestured
into the sky, his voice

a hoarse brushwork, wistful

I have always worked hard—why?

(*Ōgata Kenzan,* Autumn Ivy, *hanging scroll*)

FLOCK OF CRANES

In each eye: the unblinking clarity
of a target to whose center

the arrow flies, as if drawn there

by a gaze so calm, so steady
it has absorbed the particular world

the artist might have rendered—

mountains and clouds
a marsh, an endangered plain

of ripening grasses—

but chose not to
having met their rapt eyes directly

and understood the Source, given here

as an expanse of stunning gold
out of whose depthless depths

the cranes appear, prancing and preening

Each tapered neck so supple
it can undulate or loop

veer and aver, or lift and stay

motionless in immaculate
meditation

Consider the strict beak

the iron gaze that has seen
its true nature

and burned through it

And the blaze at the crest
so like the rising sun on the rim of the sea

or a wound blood red and mortal

In the midst of the flock
one crane has stretched wide

its black-tipped wings—

it is busking and bowing
reaching its long neck to the heights

as if already it can hear

a radiant summons, French horn gold
And now sun

gilds the great wind and snow of their going

(Ishida Yūtei, Flock of Cranes, *six-panel screen*)

for the Master of the Cranes

DRIFTING BOAT

During the banquet
what poem can I say for him
as the wine cup comes
floating by on the winding
waters? I am not a stone

in the garden, nor
an oak, nor a stalwart line
of night-mooring rocks
Not a ship held at anchor
nor the treasure sought at sea

I am what it means
to wander—*Ukifune*
a boat long adrift
in the sound of dark water
Outside the house at Uji

where I have been put
I hear rain-swept hills calling
and the cry of deer
the rush of water falling
the slow tolling of a bell

Who is it that hears?
So smoothly, so smoothly glides
my boat, that were I
to merge with the winter sea
would there be any ripple?

Snow falls on cedars
Snow melts from the bough also
Who is it that hears
the torrential ebb and flow
in the heart? In wine? In snow?

(Ukifune, *album leaf from* The Tale of Genji)

THE GIANT SNOWBALL

So sequestered and refined
a woman's life at court

she might be glimpsed
in summer

only by the fitful light
of fireflies

Her winter pastime
yukikorogashi—

gathering snow into a silver bowl
But now, carried away

by untoward gaiety
three young girls have formed

a snowball so immense
they cannot compass it, shape it

nor paint it like a rice cake
In a world of miniature hills

and artificial lakes
it's hopelessly out of scale

One can almost hear
the silence

at the center of the maiden's brimming laughter

as they pat it, stepping shyly back
as if it were a risen moon—

whose light shines equally
on the sere and the swollen

By spring the snow will
melt undone

For now, it verifies the inner eye
and keeps the balance true

*(Album leaf, from a set of twenty-four scenes
from* The Tale of Genji*)*

WILD DUCK

It ruffles
its feathers

Silent, unsleeping

the snow
descends

on bare branch
and pond

Its coal-black eyes
are bottomless

How clear
the air

How cold

(Andō Hiroshige, Wild Duck in
the Snow, *wood-block print)*

KINRYUZAN TEMPLE AT ASAKUSA

Snow
on the eaves of the temple

On parasols and shoulders

Snow above, snow below
the great lantern

at the temple's entry gate

Since the world
is beyond understanding

let it rest within

without any arrangement
of rapture

or response
Neither pain, nor penance

The courtyard
is completely white

No trace of footsteps
never mind

the icy crunch
of sandals

No wind in the tall pines
The pure

silence of the temple bell

*(Andō Hiroshige, wood-block print, from the series
"One Hundred Famous Views of Edo")*

GIFT

Winter solstice, snowmelt

Dun and lichen
the hide of the earth is

the dark, furrowed sound
of slow water off the roof

Is a worn tapestry, threadbare
at the edges of the cedars

But here inside, by the window

a stalk of flowering
moth orchid

gives itself to the sun. Each flower
is a full assent, is a festival of

readiness, is all
color brought openly to bear

on the weight of the world

A magenta so vivid
I shiver. Yes

I had wanted to rest—but rest
is just this quiet

tumult in the body's
own blossom, that turns the sky

to avalanche, and ocean

FOX FIRE AT THE CHANGING TREE

The burning that must
have been coming from me—

these are lines I'm stealing
from someone else's poem, just after

I've resolved not to lie, not to steal
to live in my evergreen

integrity as long as I can manage it
I'm much like these foxes

gathered on a night whose stars
might be flakes of snow

They have their burning torches
to lift and bear

down the road, fully camouflaged
once they've put on the stolen forms

of pious pilgrims
The bare, spreading tree above them

is fit for owls to inhabit
when a savory hunger makes them take

deadly aim
on any small rustle in the dry leaves

That's their true nature
however haunting their melancholy cries

But the foxes—for the love of me
(and it's exactly that)

I can't see why
I shouldn't want to touch them, stroke them

I might just rub the ruddy silk
of their coats against my cheek

And often have, you tell me bluntly
That friction, however

slight, sufficient to make me
spit fire, gnash my teeth

and lunge for the soft parts of your body
lifting my chin moments after

to say hotly, *I didn't mean to*
I didn't sense it coming

As if I were the innocent one
blind-sided, bloodied

(Andō Hiroshige, Fox Fire at the Changing Tree on
New Year's Eve at Ōji, *wood-block print, from the
series "One Hundred Famous Views of Edo")*

COMING AND GOING

The great horned owl slips over
the yard, its shadow half grass

half hull of old snow

Evening mist in the orchard
ripens slowly in my heart

ROUND AND ROUND THE ENTRY SCREEN

They circle the rising sun on the screen
They circle the towering wave

a great roaring of no-sound

around which they chase each other
bound and free

now you see me, now you don't
catch me if you can

don't catch me

Just ahead of the boy
trails the flowing train of his mother's

silk kimono, on which
lotus float in a dark sea of stars

The child, if he's wise, will run and run

until he enters that sea, splashing first
his face—the one before he was born

Then plunge into the depths

She knows what she's about
this elusive

mother of us all

(Isoda Koryūsai, A Happy New Year, *hanging scroll)*

WOMAN RESTING ON A BUNDLE OF KINDLING

She has squatted down
on her sore haunches to rest
Her chin on her arms
arms folded on the toppled
bundles of kindling, her only

harvest, and that too heavy
Her hands are inside
the sleeves of her kimono
as if held close to a fire
to the very source of fire

and its blossoming
She's allowed her eyes to close
Oh, but do not think
she dreams of horses to lift
her beyond the far mountains

awash with blue mist
A moment's rest, limitless
as wild Kyūshu
(the wasteland she is given
to glean) will more than suffice

How intimately
how deeply she knows the heart
That it may falter
but does not cease to open
Is dormant, then leafs out green

Whenever I am barren
sated with pleasure or grief
I enter her heart
and know its life is the one
I choose over and over

(Woman Resting on a Bundle of Kindling,
artist unknown)

*N*otes

Many of the poems in this book began with my looking at the Japanese art reproduced in *Art of Japan: A Celebration,* an art book and engagement book published by the Metropolitan Museum of Art and edited by Barbara Ford (2001). Some of my notes below rely on information she gives so succinctly in that book, which was for me a daily contemplative focus.

For details of ancient court life, I have relied principally on *Diaries of Court Ladies of Old Japan,* translated by Annie Shepley Omori and Kochi Doi, with an introduction by Amy Lowell (1920), and on *The World of the Shining Prince: Court Life in Ancient Japan,* by Ivan Morris (1964).

I wish to thank all my companions at Ocean Zendo, particularly Isshin Muryo Roshi, Dai-en, Doshin, Ryugin, Kuge, Jampa, Jishin, Engu, Ko-I, Baika, Jinen, Jittoku, Gyoji, Kenko, Kanzan, Zenki, Ryutan, and Laurel.

"Noh Robe"   The lines in italics echo the opening lines of the fourteenth-century Noh play *Sotoba Komachi:*

> In the worn-down mountains are secret places
> in the worn-down mountains are hidden places,
> but the true depths, surely, are in the human heart.

See Jane Hirshfield, *Nine Gates: Entering the Mind of Poetry* (1997), for a moving discussion of this play.

"Japanese White-Eyes"   This poem, as well as **"Mimizuku"** and **"The Tao of Love,"** comes from *Momo-chidori*, a book of illustrations and comic poems of thirty-one syllables each, called kyoka. The poems play on the names of birds.

"Baika"   *Baika* means "plum blossoms"; in street slang, a prostitute. The line in italic is taken from Zen Master Dogen.

"Summer Birds and Flowers (II)"   As Daido Loori tells us in *Invoking Reality* (1998) the word for "refuge" in Japanese, *kie-ei,* does not mean "protection" or "safe harbor." *Kie* means to act without thought of oneself, without hesitation—the way a parent rescues a child. *Ei* suggests reliance and trust. The word *refuge* in this poem, as in **"Poem Beginning with an Image of Fireflies"** and in **"The Great Wave at Kanagawa,"** is used in just this spirit of *kie-ei.*

"Poem Beginning with an Image of Fireflies"   The phrase "one bright pearl" is also from Zen Master Dogen:

> All the universe is one bright pearl
> the original face and the enlightened eye

> The mind is not I, coming and going
> in the Black Mountain's cave of demons

"Girl with Violin"   A *kicho* is a six-foot portable screen supporting opaque hangings.

"Kimono with Cricket Cages in Moonlight"   Izumi Shikibu is considered the greatest of the Japanese women poets. Fully part of life at the imperial court, she abandoned her husband for the empress' son and after his death became the lover of his brother Prince Atsumichi. After his death, she took many lovers before marrying a second time. Jane Hirshfield and Mariko Aritani offer the following translation of one of her poems:

> Although I try
> to hold the single thought

of Buddha's teaching in my heart,
I cannot help but hear
the many crickets' voices calling as well.

A *sudare* is a bamboo curtain.

"Evening Mist"   The line in italic is derived from an old Japanese verse:

I look beyond;
Flowers are not,
Nor tinted leaves.
On the sea beach
A solitary cottage stands
In the waning light
Of an autumn eve.

"Mimizuku"   The Japanese word for "owl," *mimizuku,* means "without ears," hence deaf or indifferent.

"Yamauba to Kintoki"   Yamauba is an archetypal wild woman, Kintoki a lusty infant, here wearing the long-nosed mask of a goblin "of legendary craftiness and cupidity" (Ford).

"The Hag Ibaragi"   In the Noh play *Rashomon,* Ibaragi's arm is cut off in combat by a warrior defending Kyoto from her venomous mischief. A *misu* is a thin bamboo curtain, more finely woven than a *sudare.*

"The Tao of Love"   The Japanese word for "robin" is *komadori,* a word that makes a close play on a homophonic verb that means "to be unbearably troubled" (Ford). *Wu-wei:* do nothing.

"Fox Wedding"   In Asian folklore, the fox is a trickster, "occultly nasty," according to Robert Aitken, who reports that in Japan fox shrines are visited and offerings made so that the foxes will leave people alone. The artist Ukita Ikkei satirizes a marriage of political convenience.

"Japanese Chrysanthemums"   Jittoku and Kanzan are two irrepressible iconoclasts of Zen legend, Kanzan a poet-recluse, Jittoku an orphan. They appear in a famous painting by Kaihoku Yusho.

"Drifting Boat" Ukifune is kept by Kaoru as his mistress in a lonely house by the Uji River. She is visited there by Prince Niou, who enters her bed pretending to be Kaoru. Stanza 4 echoes a note Ukifune leaves behind when she has supposedly drowned herself in the river.

"Fox Fire at the Changing Tree" Legend has it that foxes gather on New Year's Day to assume the forms of pilgrims who will then visit the Oji-Inari shrine, sacred to the fox deity (Ford).

"Woman Resting on a Bundle of Kindling" The only poem in this book inspired by a print that is not to be found in the Metropolitan Museum of Art. It hangs in my bedroom.